Behind the Glamour

BEHIND [THE] SCENES
MUSIC CAREERS

Mary Boone

raintree

a Capstone company — publishers for children

Raintree is an imprint of Capstone Global Library Limited, a company incorporated in England and Wales having its registered office at 264 Banbury Road, Oxford, OX2 7DY – Registered company number: 6695582

www.raintree.co.uk
myorders@raintree.co.uk

Editor: Alison Deering
Designers: Heidi Thompson and Kayla Rossow
Picture researcher: Pam Mitsakos
Production specialist: Tori Abraham
Originated by Capstone Global Library Ltd
Printed and bound in India

ISBN 978 1 4747 3813 2 (hardback)
20 19 18 17 16
10 9 8 7 6 5 4 3 2 1

ISBN 978 1 4747 3816 3 (paperback)
21 20 19 18 17
10 9 8 7 6 5 4 3 2 1

British Library Cataloguing in Publication Data
A full catalogue record for this book is available from the British Library.

Acknowledgements
We would like to thank the following for permission to reproduce photographs: Image Credits: Alamy: Andrew Lloyd, 28 bottom right, REUTERS, 47 top left; Dreamstime: Antoniodiaz, 43; Getty Images: Alex Mares-Manton, 5, Daniel Boczarski, 23 bottom left, Dean Mitchell, 59, Emma McIntyre, 23 middle right, Henrik Sorensen, 31 bottom right, Izabela Habur, 36, Jenny Anderson, 25, Kate Mitchell, 34, Lucidio Studio Inc., 17 top right , Marcus Lyon, 22 top right, Robert Altman, 28 top right, Robin Little, 28 middle left, Smith Collection, 56 top right; iStockphoto: AJ_Watt, 61 bottom left, 61 bottom middle, andresr, 22 top left, 24, Robert Ingelhart, cover bottom, 6 bottom; Newscom: JIM RUYMEN/UPI, 53 bottom left, KGC-243/ starmaxinc.com, 16 bottom; Shutterstock: antb, cover top right, arek_malang, 11 top left, 44 top left, Billion Photos, 9 bottom right, BlueSkyImage, 17 top left, dboystudio, 57 bottom right, Diego Cervo, 29, Evgeny Drablenkov, 20, Featureflash Photo Agency, 53 middle right, Komsan Somthi, 14, Kzenon, 17 top middle, Maksym Dykha, 9 bottom left, mama_mia, 38, Mega Pixel, 41 top right, melis, cover top left, back cover top, michaeljung, 44 top right, 45 top left, Monkey Business Images, 40, oliveromg, 61 bottom right, Pavel L Photo and Video, 50 bottom middle, Prach Trapmanee, 7 top left, Pressmaster, 49, rangizzz, 58 right, Rohappy, 13 left, Roman Voloshyn, 1, s_bukley, 53 top left, Shelly Wall, 39, Stock image, 57 bottom left, Trybex, 7 top right, Twin Design, 55 bottom left, TZIDO SUN, 10, wavebreakmedia, 45 top right, withGod, 54, YORIK, 32 top; Thinkstock: Digital Vision, 19, 35 bottom left, Plush Studios, 8

Design Elements: Shutterstock: 1nana1, 32 pixels, Andrey Nyunin, anigoweb, GeniusKp, helen-light, optimarc, Rachael Arnott, Sergey Nivens, Svetlana Prikhnenko, tele52

Contents

Introduction

On the surface, rock stars have it all. They tour the world and perform to sold-out crowds. They have fans screaming their names and singing along to their latest hits. They sign autographs, attend red-carpet events and mingle with other celebrities. But this always-in-the-spotlight lifestyle isn't for everyone. The good news is the music industry offers a wide range of jobs that are both challenging and rewarding – ones that don't come with hassles like dodging the paparazzi.

Whether you're drawn to the idea of working with high-tech equipment in a recording studio or dream of wrangling with studio executives to get your client the biggest record deal ever signed, there's a job for you in the music industry – if you're willing to work for it. Even if you're working behind the glamour, there is intense competition at all levels within the music industry. Don't be discouraged. Simply figure out how to get the training and experience needed to set yourself apart. In many cases, you'll need to start as an intern or in an entry-level job. This will help you gain hands-on familiarity with the business. The more you learn, the more connections you make, and the harder you work, the better your chances of landing your dream job.

First things first – decide if music is where your passion lies. If it is, start researching jobs and considering your own strengths. If you know someone in the music business – even a member of a small, local band – ask if you can observe and learn what he or she does. Watch the crew as they set up microphones and soundboards. Stay around for soundcheck and help pack up equipment after a show. Every experience will help you decide if this is the field for you and which aspect of it interests you most.

According to a 2012 survey by LinkedIn, a business-oriented social networking service, 30 per cent of workers around the world say they are earning a living from their childhood dream job or a related field.

BIG MONEY BEHIND THE GLAMOUR

Sure, stars such as Adele and Justin Bieber are hauling in big paychecks, but plenty of behind-the-scenes players in the music industry are millionaires too. For instance:

• Music producer Rick Rubin cofounded Def Jam Records and is former co-president of Columbia Records. He's produced records for artists including the Beastie Boys, Kanye West and Jay Z. Rubin has a net worth of £320 million.

• Bernie Taupin is an English lyricist best known for his long-term collaboration with Elton John. Taupin's net worth is approximately £46 million.

• Clive Calder is a South African record executive and businessman primarily known for co-founding the Zomba Group and Jive Records. Calder has a net worth of £2 billion.

CHAPTER 1

Audio engineer

If you're equal parts musician and computer nerd, audio engineering may be the perfect fit for you. It's a field that requires both a trained ear and comfort with complex equipment. Professional audio engineers are responsible for operating and maintaining sound-recording or broadcast equipment. As an audio engineer, you could be in charge of placing microphones and speakers, setting sound levels, conducting soundchecks and correcting any problems along the way.

Audio engineers may also oversee live mixing of sound for concerts or recording projects. Mixing is the process by which sound from multiple sources is combined. Much of this work is done under tight time constraints, making it a high-pressure job.

If you want to be an audio engineer, you also need to have good communication and people skills. These will be essential when working with musicians, film or TV directors, editors, video technicians and others, all of whom want the best possible sound.

Some audio engineers get to work for large concert tours or other touring performances. If you love to travel, that might be a good fit for you. You'll also need to be flexible. Setting up a show in a different city every few nights means adapting to changing schedules and processes.

So what can you do to get into this field? Successful audio engineers often attend two-year training programmes before landing their first jobs in the industry. You'll likely start out as an audio technician running errands, connecting microphones and speakers, and tracking down problems with audio signals. From there, you might be promoted to an assistant audio engineer position. You'll continue to do set-up and teardown work but also take on other responsibilities, such as maintaining the tape library. Skilled assistant audio engineers might eventually find work as audio engineers. They'll continue to take on engineering duties, as well as manage recording projects or live sessions, assign tasks to assistants and interact with clients.

A passion for music often drives audio engineers to dedicate their time and energy to this career, but you should still be prepared to work hard. Some audio engineers work full-time for a specific studio, musical artist or theatre, while others work for themselves and take on freelance projects.

At a glance

The basics: Audio engineer

Also known as: Sound engineer, recording engineer

Overview: Audio engineers work in recording studios and operate equipment to record, synchronize, mix, or reproduce music, voices or sound effects.

Suggested courses: Music, computer science, electronics

Salary range: £18,020 – £94,860/year with an average salary of £42,690/year

INSIDE THE BIZ WITH JOEY STURGIS

Joey Sturgis is an experienced audio engineer, producer, mixer, co-writer and collaborator for bands who play music festivals such as the Warped Tour, Soundwave, Loud Park Japan, Alternative Press and Kerrang!

Q: How did you first get into this field?

A: I started as a musician who played in a band, and I wanted a recording of myself so I learned how to do it on my own. Soon after that, other bands would listen to my recordings and ask me to record them... I decided to give it a shot, and I turned out to be pretty good at it... It was fun and challenging all the same!

Q: What personality traits should someone have if they want to become an audio engineer?

A: Patience and determination

Q: What's the most challenging aspect of your job?

A: Working well with people and prioritizing their needs over yours

Q: What's the most rewarding part of your job?

A: Satisfying an audience at large and seeing the fans love the songs

Q: What's your best advice for someone thinking about becoming an audio engineer?

A: One of the most important things you need to know ... is that you're literally creating history... That, in and of itself, is a very important task... Music is all about conveying emotion and message, and half the battle is translating the artist's emotion and message into a viable product, without damaging the integrity of the art.

Girl power

Women account for just 5 per cent of those working in music production and the recording arts, but Karrie Keyes is hoping to change that. She joined with Michelle Sabolchick Pettinato to create Soundgirls.org. This nonprofit organization provides support to women working in audio and girls who are considering getting into the business. The all-volunteer organization began holding summer recording camps for girls in 2015. They hope to expand the program in years to come.

"Nobody knows why there are so few women in the field," says Keyes. "A lot of it probably is because young girls don't even know it's an option. That's too bad, because it's a really challenging and exciting field for someone who is drawn to music."

Keyes says many colleges and universities offer practical training in audio engineering, but adds that there are many things about the business that you can only learn by doing it.

"...hands-on experience is crucial ... I always tell everyone to find a mentor and learn everything you can from them," she says. "That's one of the main reasons we founded SoundGirls, so more experienced members can be a resource to less experienced members.

SoundGirls.org has 2,000 members around the world. You can sign up for a free membership at www.soundgirls.org

CHAPTER 2

Songwriter

Songwriters, obviously, write songs. And if you love storytelling, poetry and music, a career as a songwriter might be perfect for you! But there's more to this behind-the-scenes career than just writing songs. It's important to understand the distinction between a songwriter and a lyricist. Lyricists write lyrics only – as a songwriter, you'll be responsible for creating the entire song, both the lyrics and the melody.

How and where a songwriter works may differ depending upon his or her particular skill set. Some songwriters work for themselves and then try to sell their songs to record companies or musicians. Others work as full-time employees at music publishers, advertising agencies or record companies. Record company songwriters are often assigned to write for specific artists or bands. The companies need writers who can produce songs suited to a musician's voice or style. A good songwriter – and a good relationship between a songwriter and musician – allows the musician to keep putting out hits.

No matter where they work, all songwriters must start with an idea and a thorough understanding of the message they're trying to convey. Many songwriters write lyrics first and then write the music to accompany it. Others come up with a melody and add words later.

Once a song is complete, you'll need to produce a demo. Demos are recordings songwriters use to try to sell a song. In order to successfully pitch your song and demo, it's important to have strong people skills. You may want to take public-speaking classes to help you gain confidence when presenting your songs to record label executives, artists, producers and managers.

Another essential skill for a songwriter is the ability to play an instrument – after all, you'll need to actually strum the chords or play the keys while creating songs. Passion and knowledge of the music industry are also essential. Successful songwriters often explore multiple music styles and genres. Many songwriters also perform music, so a good portion of their time may be spent touring, collaborating with other artists or recording.

Many songwriters only dream of scoring a single hit song, but there's one who has outdone all others – Paul McCartney. According to the *Guinness Book of World Records*, McCartney is credited as the songwriter on 32 chart-topping hits on the US charts and 29 hits in the United Kingdom.

At a glance

The Basics: Songwriter

Also known as: Writer, lyricist

Overview: Songwriters craft songs for themselves and for other artists. Songwriters typically write both the lyrics and melody for a song; lyricists exclusively write lyrics.

Suggested courses: Guitar or piano lessons, poetry, music theory, sound engineering or recording classes, speech

Salary range: £12,160 – £71,070/year with an average salary of £32,020/year; many songwriters work on a per-project basis.

INSIDE THE BIZ WITH ANJI KAT

Anji Kat worked in the health and wellness industry for 20 years before deciding to pursue her real passion — music — in 2011. The award-winning singer/songwriter now lives and works in Clearwater, Florida, USA.

Q: How did you first get into this field?

A: I loved writing poetry since I was a kid, and I also loved singing. I started putting the two together and writing songs. When I started singing at church and at coffee shops and received positive feedback, I discovered how much I wanted it to be my career.

Q: What personality traits should someone have if they want to become a songwriter?

A: Creativity, ability to focus, and discipline to get projects done. Passion for music, and specifically writing, are essential.

Q: What's the most challenging aspect of your job?

A: Creative jobs, such as songwriting, do not easily fit within a traditional 9 a.m. to 5 p.m. workday. Productivity and work output can fluctuate wildly... Some days you'll write songs easily, and some days you will find it hard to write anything. Additionally, there is a lot to the business side of being a songwriter that can feel discouraging to new writers if they are trying to get their work published.

Q: What's the most rewarding part of your job?

A: I love music and writing songs that really touch people's hearts or make them think. I love the creative aspect of it and telling a story in different ways.

CHAPTER 3

Music producer

Do you love music and like being in charge? If so, you might have a future as a music producer. Music producers are the bosses of the recording process. They gather ideas and songs for a project, hire and coach studio musicians, control the recording sessions, supervise the mixing process, manage schedules and budgets and negotiate contracts.

Producers employed by large studios may work more like directors on film sets, telling others what they need to do to make a great recording. Music producers working for themselves or with smaller studios often take a more hands-on approach. They actually arrange or rearrange music, set microphones, run computer software and even play some of the instruments.

Regardless of where they work, all producers strive to bring their own creative touches to their projects. The resulting songs and albums often have such distinctive sounds that a producer may become as associated with the music as the artist. Max Martin, for example, has produced hits for acts including the Backstreet Boys, NSYNC, Britney Spears, Katy Perry and Taylor Swift. The songs he produces are all different, but they all have his signature melodic touch in them.

The best music producers understand and balance the artistic value of music with the commercial appeal that goes into creating a hit song. Producers must be true to the artist's creative vision and coax the best possible performance out of the artist. The producer is then responsible for moulding that vision and performance into a song that record studio executives can sell to the public.

Producers don't necessarily have to be musicians, but a good producer must have a solid understanding of music and music trends. Additionally, producers need to be skilled at project management, including the ability to work with creative people, meet deadlines and stay on budget.

Many universities and colleges offer classes in music production, but even with a degree from a top university, you'll likely need to start in an entry-level job and work your way up.

If music producing interests you, it's never too early to start making contact with people working as producers. Try to connect with a producer who works either freelance or for a small studio and ask if you can job shadow him or her. The connections you make could eventually lead to an internship or your first job.

DID YOU KNOW?

Audiophile is the term used to describe someone passionate about high-quality sound reproduction.

At a Glance

The basics: Music producer

Also known as: Producer, record producer

Overview: Music producers are the visionaries for the overall sound and feel of an album or single; they work to help musicians create the best possible final product.

Suggested courses: Music, technology, economics/business, writing, broadcasting

Salary range: £16,000 — £800,500+/year with an average salary of £44,000/year

PRODUCERS BEHIND THE HITS

You know artists such as Taylor Swift and Miley Cyrus, but do you know the producers behind their hits? Music producers add creative touches to songs that set them apart from others. They coach artists, they take risks and, when it all works, they make hits. These three music producers' work has topped the charts:

1. Dann Huff — Huff got his start as a 1980s rock guitarist. These days, he's a hit-making producer who has worked with artists including Keith Urban, Rascal Flatts, Faith Hill and Tim McGraw. He says the secret to producing hits is to ask the artists lots of questions and to focus on what they care about.

2. Max Martin — This Swedish producer got his start in the 1990s, writing and producing hits for Ace of Base, Backstreet Boys, NSYNC and Britney Spears. More recently, he's worked with superstars including Maroon 5, Taylor Swift and Katy Perry.

3. Michael Len Williams II — Known professionally as Mike Will Made It, Williams started working in the business when he was 17 years old. He has since produced hits with dozens of artists including Lil Wayne, Drake, Kelly Rowland, Rihanna, Miley Cyrus, Ciara, Beyoncé, Ludacris and Future.

CHAPTER 4

Session musician

If you love playing a wide range of music and dream of working with a variety of artists, a career as a session musician may be the perfect choice for you. Session musicians back other artists during live performances or on recordings. And whether you're a vocalist or an instrumentalist, working as a session musician will allow you to use your talents in a wide range of situations.

Session musicians are typically hired one job at a time, meaning they're not on the regular payroll of the artist or studio doing the hiring. For example, a band may want to feature a saxophone on a particular song, but no one in the band plays sax. The band could hire a session musician to record the part and contribute to the arrangement. If that song becomes a hit, the session musician could be hired to join the band's tour for several months or even a year.

Being a session musician means being flexible. Skilled session musicians may find work with a pop star one day and a country musician the next. Because they're always backing different musicians with different styles, it pays to be well versed in a wide range of musical styles and genres. It's helpful to know how to sight-read music, improvise or play several instruments – the more instruments you play, the more employment opportunities you're likely to find.

In addition to being flexible and talented, session musicians must be responsible and respectful. You need to show up on time, offer constructive input when asked for it, and remember that your ability to seamlessly fit into any setting will largely influence whether or not you get hired again.

Networking is also an important part of being a session musician. You need to contact studios, artists and even friends and family to let them know you're available for session work. Most session musicians start out small, sometimes playing for free for artists who need the help. Keep in mind that every job – paid or not – helps gain experience and builds the reputation needed to get to the next step in this very competitive field.

At a glance

The basics: Session musician

Also known as: Studio musician, backup musician

Overview: Session musicians — instrumentalists or vocalists — perform backing tracks for another musician onstage or on recordings; most work with many different artists and bands.

Suggested courses: Music lessons, economics/business, marketing

Salary range: £7.50 — £55.22/hour with an average salary of £19.37/hour. Musicians are typically self-employed.

INSIDE THE BIZ WITH KAREEM KANDI

Kareem Kandi is a performer, composer and educator based in Tacoma, Washington, USA. Kandi, who plays saxophone, flute, clarinet and piano, has worked as a session musician, recorded with The Paperboys, and played shows with artists including Patti Labelle, Ali Jackson, Bill Watrous and others.

Q: What personality traits should someone have if they want to become a session musician?

A: You have to have a good attitude. If you're difficult to work with, you're not going to go very far.

Q: What's the most challenging aspect of your job?

A: There's a lot of sitting around, waiting for engineers to get the sound just right or maybe you have to do multiple takes. It takes a lot of time to get everything just right.

Q: What's the most rewarding part of your job?

A: I enjoy working with other artists, and it's pretty awesome to hear the finished product. I do a lot of shows, but with a recording it's there forever, and I like that.

Q: What's your best advice for someone thinking about becoming a session musician?

A: You need to be able to sight-read music very well. You also need to be able to improvise, so you should get comfortable with that. No matter how young you are, you should start recording, even if it's just on your phone. Listen to all styles of music, get to know people in the business and ask if you can hang around when they're performing or recording. You'll learn a lot just being around other musicians.

CELEBS WHO WERE SESSION MUSICIANS

Stardom doesn't always come quickly or easily. Here are a few examples of artists who worked as session musicians before making it big:

- Pianist Billy Preston had an impressive solo career, winning a Grammy in 1972 for his instrumental soundtrack "Outa-Space." Before he became famous — and even after he did — he worked as a session musician for artists including Little Richard, Ray Charles, The Beatles, The Rolling Stones and The Red Hot Chili Peppers.

- British singer-songwriter and instrumentalist Eska Mtungwazi, who plays guitar, violin and piano, received a 2015 Mercury Music Prize for her debut album. Before going out on her own, she performed as a session musician on more than 150 releases, including projects with Zero 7, Nitin Sawhney, Grace Jone and Bobby McFerrin.

- Before Glen Campbell became a country-pop superstar, he was one of the industry's most in-demand session guitarists. His talents were featured on recordings by artists including The Beach Boys, Frank Sinatra and The Monkees.

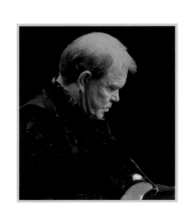

CHAPTER 5

A&R representative

Do you love scoping out the coolest newest bands before anyone else has even heard of them? Are you the one telling your friends about the hottest new singles? Do you love attending live shows? If the idea of searching for the next big thing sounds appealing, perhaps you're suited for a career as an A&R representative.

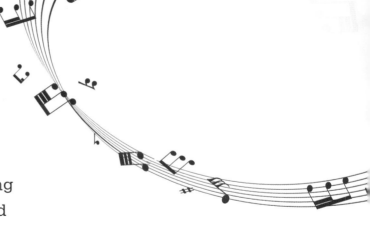

A&R, which stands for artists and repertoire, is the division of a record label responsible for scouting talent. A&R reps listen to demos and attend shows, always looking for artists who have the potential to be commercially successful.

After an A&R rep signs someone to the label, he or she continues to work with the artist, serving as an advisor. As an A&R rep, it's up to you to make sure each musician is partnered with the right producer, help select songs and fine tune an artist's look and sound. You'll also help determine how the artist will be marketed and, at some smaller labels, try to get your artist's music placed in TV shows or on commercials. You'll also serve as a musician's point of contact at the label during contract negotiations.

A&R is a very competitive field. Most A&R reps have degrees in marketing, business, communications or music business. After completing these studies, you'll likely start off by finding a position as an intern in order to gain industry experience. Many A&R reps also start off as A&R administrators before working their way up to scouting talent.

The life and career of an A&R rep is fast-paced. You should expect to juggle many different projects at the same time. Late nights at shows or in the studio are commonplace. But it's not a job where you can sleep all day and work at night. Record producers, artists and other executives expect to be able to meet with the reps during daytime hours.

The best A&R reps know a lot about music, music history and music trends. They read music publications and know the best places to hear new music. They can see potential in acts that still need a lot of polish. Additionally, they are great communicators, open to meeting new people, and are comfortable working as a go-between for the label and the artist. If that sounds like you, you just might have a future as an A&R rep.

At a glance

The basics: A&R rep

Also known as: A&R scout, A&R staffer, A&R coordinator

Overview: Artists & repertoire reps scout for new talent, then work with those artists to help them develop into commercial successes.

Suggested courses: Music, creative writing, economics/business, marketing, psychology

Salary range: £14,400 — £68,000/year with an average salary of £40,000/year

INSIDE THE BIZ WITH JOY STRINGER

Joy Stringer is the director of A&R and marketing for Crucial Music Corporation in Los Angeles. A lifelong music fan, she's been finding leads for Crucial's roster of artists for four years.

Q: What personality traits are essential for an A&R rep?
A: You should be open to meeting a lot of new people, organized and good at multitasking. You also need to be patient, because artists tend to work on their own time schedules.

Q: What's the most challenging aspect of your job?
A: We work with a large number of artists, so it can be challenging to juggle everyone and make each artist feel valued. I also find it challenging to have to tell people no. It's hard to disappoint people, especially when they are passionate about their music.

Q: What's the most rewarding part of your job?
A: It's amazing when we are able to place someone's music in a TV programme that they already watch and love. It is also very rewarding when an artist tells us that their album sales have jumped after we placed one of their songs in a film or TV show.

Q: What's your best advice for someone thinking about becoming an A&R rep?
A: Listen to as much music as you can in many different genres. Listen to old music so you can hear how it has influenced today's music. Ask your parents who they listened to when they were your age... Ask your grandparents the same!

CHAPTER 6

Music publicist

Are you a pro at spreading the word about the coolest new band before anyone else has heard of them? If so, a career as a music publicist might be the perfect fit for you. Music publicists are press agents or public relations specialists who focus on getting press for musical acts. They are an artist's link to the media.

Music publicists may work for record companies, public relations agencies or for an individual artist. Most of the time, publicists are concerned with getting press coverage of a musician's new concert tour, shows or albums. To do that, they write press releases, compile lists of media contacts, create press kits, schedule interviews and send out albums for review. All of these things are crucial to getting the word out to fans. After all, it's impossible to buy tickets to a show you don't know about or purchase an album from a band you've never heard of.

Occasionally, music publicists are called upon to help manage media coverage of an artist's private life, such as an engagement, divorce or the birth of a child. Publicists may also speak on behalf of their clients. They advise artists whether they should speak to the media or simply say, "No comment." Taylor Swift's publicist, for example, has been called upon many times to answer questions about the pop star's relationships. Is she distraught over a breakup? Is she dating someone new? Is it serious? Her publicist can respond – or not – to those sorts of questions on Swift's behalf.

A good music publicist is also a people person. After all, a publicist's job is dependent on building and maintaining relationships with the media. A reporter who doesn't like or respect a publicist may choose not to write about the musician or may opt to only focus on the negative. If you're looking to get into this field, you should be outgoing, friendly and comfortable meeting new people.

So how can you get into public relations? Most music publicists have degrees in fields such as public relations, marketing, advertising, journalism, communications or music business. Strong oral and written communication skills are crucial, as are organization and the ability to meet deadlines. Expect to start out as an intern or publicity assistant and work your way up before landing a job as a publicist.

At a glance

The basics: Music publicist

Also known as: Press agent, public relations agent, PR specialist, spokesperson

Overview: Music publicists represent artists to the broadcast, print and online media.

Suggested courses: English, journalism, public relations, marketing, advertising, creative writing

Salary range: £25,370 – £88,120/year with an average salary of £45,450/year

The music business is a very big business. According to analysts at Spotify, the global music business was worth more than £20 billion at the end of 2015.

BEING SOCIAL

A strong social media presence is key to gaining publicity. In fact, many artists and record companies have members of their publicity teams devoted entirely to creating or maintaining their social media presence. These publicists don't worry about talking to newspaper reporters or DJs. Instead, they make sure the artist is connecting with fans via Facebook, Instagram, Twitter, Flickr, Vimeo, YouTube, Pinterest, SnapChat and Ning.

Some artists may manage their own social networks, but because the Internet never sleeps, it can be all-consuming to try to respond to fans' comments and keep material fresh. Social media managers write and post compelling material on an artist's networks so musicians can stay connected without having to take their focus off creating music.

CHAPTER 7

Music journalist

If the thought of interviewing music superstars and seeing your writing in the pages of *Rolling Stone* or *Variety* sounds appealing, a career as a music journalist may be perfect for you. Music journalists report on music news, the latest music releases, concerts and more. Their work may appear in print and online newspapers and magazines or in radio or television broadcasts.

As a music journalist, your job is to research artists, conduct interviews, listen to CDs, attend concerts and CD release parties, and write stories or reviews. As fun as that may sound, it's not all play. Music journalists must hustle to set up interviews, get press passes and even earn assignments. Journalists who are reviewing live performances can't sit back and enjoy the show like any other audience member. They must take notes about the song list, the stage, costuming, the sound and the crowd. Then, depending on deadlines, they must quickly – sometimes within just 20 to 30 minutes – write a review of the show.

The American Society of Composers, Authors and Publishers (ASCAP) started honouring outstanding media coverage of music in 1968 with its annual Deems Taylor Awards.

Some music journalists work full-time at specific publications, while others work as freelancers, meaning they write for a handful of different publications. Journalists working for larger or specialty media outlets often specialize in covering one type of music, such as rock or classical. Those working for smaller publications and websites are often called upon to cover all styles of music, writing about rap one day and interviewing a symphony conductor the next. Some music journalists write unbiased, factual reports about the industry. Many others write music critiques, in which they share their opinions about specific performances or recordings.

Even if college is years away, you can begin to gain experience as a music journalist by starting your own music review blog or YouTube channel. You might also consider working for your school newspaper or as an intern at a small community newspaper or radio station. Getting experience now will help you decide if this is really the career for you and, if it is, you'll already be on your way.

At a Glance

The basics: Music journalist

Also known as: Music critic, music writer, music reporter

Overview: Music journalists write music news and reviews for print, broadcast, and online media. They must be aware of trends, interview artists and attend shows.

Suggested courses: English, journalism, music, music history, technology

Salary range: £16,000 – £56,000+/year with an average salary of £34,568/year

INSIDE THE BIZ WITH HANNAH LEVIN

Hannah Levin has worked as a radio DJ/producer and as a music journalist. The Tucson, Arizona, resident has contributed articles to many publications including *The Stranger*, *BUST*, *Rolling Stone* and *SPIN*.

Q: How did you first get into this field?

A: I started out in the music industry as a band manager and then a promoter. I eventually realized that the most effective way to nurture young bands and shine a spotlight on artists was to write about them. At that point, I knew a lot of people at the local papers and just asked if I could review a record for *Seattle Weekly*. They said yes, and within a few months, I had my first cover story.

Q: What personality traits are essential for a music journalist?

A: A great deal of self-motivation and self-sufficiency. No one will hand you work, even if you're good. You also have to thrive under deadlines — that's non-negotiable. Shyness will work against you as an interviewer, so you have to have an engaging demeanor and natural curiosity to learn more about artists and their creative process.

Q: What's the most challenging aspect of your job?

A: Low pay, high pressure.

Q: What's the most rewarding part of your job?

A: Personal creative expression and being able to help others discover great music.

CHAPTER 8

Entertainment lawyer

Knowing the ins and outs of entertainment law can be a challenging job – but it can also be exciting. And if you're equally interested in law and entertainment, this could be the career for you! Entertainment lawyers provide legal advice to artists and companies involved in all areas of the entertainment industry, including film, radio, television, music, publishing, theatre, sports and multimedia entertainment. Some entertainment lawyers have generalized practices, while others specialize in a subset of the industry, such as music. But no matter what, an entertainment lawyer is responsible for representing his or her client's best interests.

Like all other lawyers, being an entertainment lawyer requires a law degree. But instead of focussing on areas such as immigration issues or property, entertainment lawyers work with musicians, record producers, songwriters, music publishers, agents and record label executives. They negotiate and review legal documents related to recording, merchandising, touring and publishing.

As an entertainment lawyer, you must know the ins and outs of contracts, as well as the laws associated with intellectual property, labour and employment and privacy rights. This knowledge will come in handy when it comes to negotiating contracts and endorsement deals, determining licensing of products, dealing with tax issues or even reviewing property contracts.

Becoming a lawyer of any kind requires years of study – both an undergraduate degree and a post-graduate degree in law are a must. While an undergraduate law degree isn't a must for becoming a lawyer, it's useful to take classes that will help educate you about the type of law you want to practise. You also need to pass the bar exam to become a practising lawyer. If you're interested in this type of law, look for a university that offers entertainment law courses.

While you're in university – either undergraduate or postgraduate – look for internships at law firms that specialize in entertainment law. After finishing university, expect to assist – or clerk – at a law firm while working your way up. You may not land a job at an entertainment law firm right away. Young lawyers start as associates, and partners direct their work. Most entertainment lawyers work at law firms or as in-house counsel at entertainment companies.

At a glance

The basics: Entertainment lawyer

Also known as: Entertainment attorney, media lawyer, arts lawyer

Overview: Entertainment lawyers manage all legal matters for clients, including reviewing contracts and negotiating recording, merchandising, touring and publishing deals. Entertainment lawyers may also help clients with copyright issues, business developments and tax/financial matters.

Suggested courses: Speech and debate, sociology, history, political science, English, creative writing, business

Salary range: £57,000 – £85,000/year with an average salary of £66,450/year

BLURRED LINES

Many of the highest-profile entertainment law cases have to do with copyright. Copyright laws keep other artists from copying all or part of an original song without permission. Some famous music copyright cases include:

- A 2015 jury found Pharrell Williams and Robin Thicke guilty of copying Marvin Gaye's "Got to Give It Up," when they wrote their song "Blurred Lines." Williams and Thicke were ordered to pay £5.8 million to Gaye's estate.

- R&B singer Jessie Braham filed a £34 million lawsuit against Taylor Swift, saying she stole her "Shake It Off" lyrics from him. In 2015, a California judge said there was not enough evidence and dismissed the case.

- In 2014, Sam Smith settled a claim that parts of his song "Stay with Me" were copied from the 1989 hit "I Won't Back Down." Smith agreed to share royalties from his song with "I Won't Back Down" songwriters Tom Petty and Jeff Lynne.

INSIDE THE BIZ WITH JUSTIN ELDRETH

Justin Eldreth has worked as a line producer and production manager for companies including HBO, TBS, NBC and AT&T. Along the way, he had lots of legal questions and had to find the answers on his own. That's what inspired him to go to law school and establish his own law practice, specializing in entertainment law, in Raleigh, North Carolina, USA.

Q: What personality traits should someone have if they want to become an entertainment lawyer?

A: Patience, abstract problem solving, critical thinking

Q: What's the most challenging aspect of your job?

A: Often clients come to my office after they have been harmed or their ideas have been stolen. My favourite clients are those who understand that an ounce of prevention is worth a pound of cure. With a little forethought and planning, a good lawyer can set you up to succeed and better protect your interests.

Q: What's the most rewarding part of your job?

A: When a client says thank you or when I get to help them prosper in their profession. For example, I represented a pro-boxer in federal court. There was an injunction against him fighting any more fights until the legal issues could be resolved. My work convinced a judge to lift the injunction, and he was allowed to fight on national television that weekend in a match in line for a title.

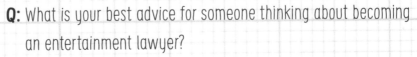

Q: What is your best advice for someone thinking about becoming an entertainment lawyer?

A: Learn the business before you learn the law. Nothing in law school will teach you how the entertainment business works and what your clients expect you to know. Context is key.

CHAPTER 9

Music manager

Are you a planner? A doer? A mover and shaker? Do you like making decisions? If you answered YES! to these questions, you might have a future as a music manager. Music managers guide the development of their artists' careers. They work hard to help clients secure recording contracts, book performances and sell records. To do that, they must be excellent strategists. They need to be able to evaluate offers and opportunities and help clients determine what fits best with their long-term career plans.

In addition to being a good strategist, a manager must be an excellent communicator. Good communication and social skills are an essential part of representing a client when dealing with booking agents, music venues and record companies. Managers must also have a solid understanding of business and contracts. For example, if an energy drink wants a musician to be its spokesperson, the musician's manager must evaluate the offer and determine if it's a good partnership. Do the product and the artist appeal to the same audience? Do they have the same values?

Is there enough financial incentive for the artist to lend her name to the product? Are there risks?

Some music managers work for management companies and handle several different artists. If an artist is successful enough, he or she may hire a manager directly. Very few managers make a regular salary; some are paid a base salary plus a percentage of what their clients make. The vast majority of management deals are based on commission. That means the manager earns a percentage, usually 10 to 20 per cent, of the income the artist generates.

Do you think you have what it takes to make it as a music manager? If so, a degree in business, communications, law or even music management is a great way to get started. Once you have a degree, the key to finding a job as a music manager is to gain experience. Many music managers begin their careers by managing a friend's band for free or for a percentage of any performances booked. They may also work as promoters, assistants, engineers or artists to learn the industry inside out before stepping into a managerial role.

At a glance

The basics: Music manager

Also known as: Artist manager, talent manager, agent

Overview: Music managers are responsible for overseeing the career development of the artists they represent.

Suggested courses: Music, maths, technology, law, business

Salary range: £22,460 — £89,160/year with an average salary of £50,390/year

INSIDE THE BIZ WITH ERIC KNIGHT

Eric Knight, president and founder of Los Angeles-based Persistent Management, has worked as an artist manager for 10 years. His company manages the careers of artists including Latin pop-rock sensation Ignacio Val and hard rock band Disciples of Babylon.

Q: How did you first get into this field?

A: I first got into artist management with the band I used to perform with. I saw that the band was playing around town, but there didn't seem to be any direction or plan for where we were headed. I decided to take the reins and start organizing our business affairs. I started reading everything I could on the subject and immersed myself on the business side. I became the band's booking agent, publicist and promoter.

Q: What's the most challenging aspect of your job?

A: ...trying to get the artist to that next level of their career. It is such a hard business to break into. There is a lot of rejection, and the word "no" is used quite a bit ... that's something you have to get used to.

Q: What's the most rewarding part of your job?

A: I like developing artists and taking them from where they are currently in their careers and building them to their full potential.

Q: What's your best advice for someone thinking about becoming an artist manager?

A: Learn everything you can... Take business courses so you understand how finances work. Ultimately the best way is to get out there and start doing it. There's nothing like the real-world experience of working with acts to begin honing your skills to become a great manager.

KEEPING IT IN THE FAMILY

Many musicians rely on a family member to manager their careers when they're just starting out. Unfortunately, that doesn't always work out.

- Actress and singer Selena Gomez made a media splash in 2014 when she fired her mother and stepfather as her managers.

- In 2000, country/pop singer LeAnn Rimes sued her father/manager for stealing £5.6 million of her earnings.

- Beyoncé fired her father as her manager in 2011. The singer says her father stole money from her, and she has threatened to take him to court over ownership of the Destiny's Child brand.

CHAPTER 10

Music supervisor

You're watching a scary film. Just as the young starlet opens the door leading to a creepy cellar, the music builds. A series of chilling minor chords let you know that danger lurks just down the stairs. Or perhaps you're watching the opening scenes of a television show when the sight of lush fields and the sound of bagpipes signal that the characters are in Scotland.

Whether you realize it or not, you're witnessing the work of a music supervisor. Music can set the scene and add emotional undertones to TV or films. If the idea of selecting that music is appealing to you, you might enjoy a career as a music supervisor.

Music supervisors work with production teams to suggest, choose, or create tracks for television, films, adverts or video games. They negotiate with businesses or individuals to secure rights to music, and they edit music and compositions. They also oversee the composers and other musicians when original music is created for a film.

In order to be a successful music supervisor, you must be knowledgeable about the technical aspects of music and how it interacts with visual media. Many music supervisors take music psychology classes and study classic films to fully grasp the impact music can make when paired with a film or TV show. Even though viewers are generally more in tune with what they're seeing on the screen than with what they're hearing, music helps create a mood without the viewer ever realizing it.

The first commercially available movie soundtrack was released in January 1938. Leigh Harline was music supervisor for the project entitled "Songs from Walt Disney's Snow White and the Seven Dwarfs."

Work as a music supervisor is interesting and varied – but it may not always be steady. Rather than working full-time for a particular studio or company, most music supervisors are paid per project. Small independent films and TV shows, for example, pay considerably less than major motion pictures.

At a glance

The basics: Music supervisor

Also known as: Music director, MXSup

Overview: Music supervisors place music in films, television shows, video games and commercials.

Suggested courses: Music, music history, marketing, psychology, business, accounting, ethics, law

Salary range: £23,200 – £54,400/year with an average salary of £35,190/year*

* Music supervisors are typically paid per project – salaries range from £1,600 – £4,000 per TV episode and £120,100 – £400,280 for a big-budget film.

If a career as a music supervisor sounds interesting to you, you'll likely want to attend a university to study music, music business or film scoring. Because music supervisors must also understand how to draft licensing agreements and obtain rights to music, law and music business courses are also useful. Look for internships both while you are studying and after graduation to gain on-the-job experience. Aspiring music supervisors often enter the industry through entry-level jobs at record companies or in the music departments of film or TV studios. These positions can help an individual make contacts while learning the business from the ground up.

MAKING MAGIC WITH MUSIC

Dave Jordan has played a starring role in more than 36 films, but chances are you've never heard of him.

Jordan isn't a leading man. He's a music supervisor. And whether you know it or not, you've heard his work on blockbuster Marvel films, including *Avengers*, the *Iron Man* films, *Captain America*, *Transformers*, *Thor*, *The Incredible Hulk*, *Fantastic Four*, *Godzilla*, *Guardians of the Galaxy*, *Ant-Man* and *Daredevil*. Jordan has also worked on *The Fast and the Furious*, *Harold & Kumar Go to White Castle* and *Dude Where's My Car?*

In total, the films Jordan has worked on have earned more than £10.7 billion. He's also won the Hollywood Music Award for Music Supervisor of the Year. Jordan got his start working for a record label. In 2001, he founded his own music supervision and publishing company, Format Entertainment.

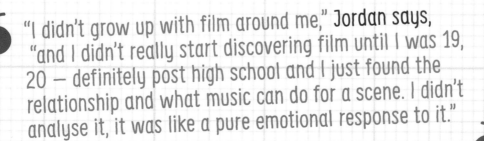

"I didn't grow up with film around me," Jordan says, "and I didn't really start discovering film until I was 19, 20 — definitely post high school and I just found the relationship and what music can do for a scene. I didn't analyse it, it was like a pure emotional response to it."

CHAPTER 11

Getting your foot in the door

So often in the music industry, experience is crucial to success. Studios and artists are reluctant to hire someone unless you have experience to back you up. But how do you gain that experience and get your foot in the door? Internships.

An internship is a period of work experience, typically lasting anywhere from a week to a year, offered by an employer to give students and new graduates exposure to the work environment. Interns are able to gain experience, often in exchange for school credit or pay, before officially entering the workforce.

TO FIND A MUSIC INTERNSHIP, FOLLOW THESE TIPS:

- Check with the career centre or advisor at your school.

- Contact recording studios, production facilities, musicians and others in the industry.

- Ask your music teachers, family members and friends; someone may have a connection that could land you a music internship.

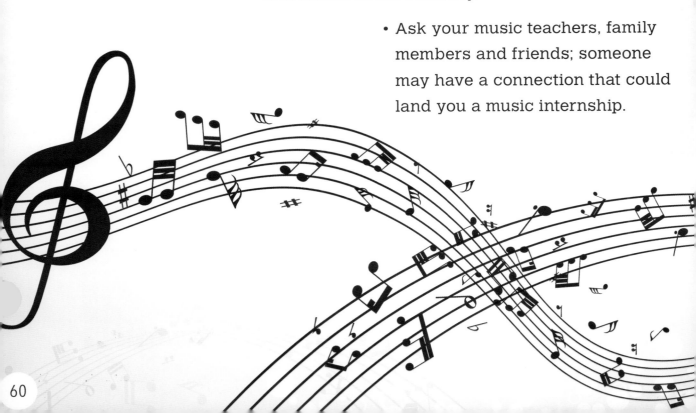

ONCE YOU LAND AN INTERNSHIP, MAKE THE MOST OF IT:

- Meet with your supervisor to set expectations for your experience.

- Present yourself in a professional way. Be on time, say "please" and "thank you," and follow through – if you say you're going to do something, do it.

- Get to know others in the company – and not just those you work with directly. It's possible that someone else is doing a job that might interest you in the future.

Keep a list of everything you do during your internship. This will help you evaluate your work when you meet with your supervisor. It will also help you remember everything you've done so you can update your CV – and eventually land a real job in the music industry.

FIND OUT MORE

Music What Job Can I Get? (I'm Good At), Richard Spilsbury (Wayland, 2015)

Recording and Promoting Your Music (I'm in the Band), Matthew Annis (Raintree, 2014)

The Story of Hip-Hop (Pop Histories), Matt Annis (Franklin Watts, 2013)

WEBSITES

www.careersinmusic.co.uk/

Learn more about a career in music and how to get your foot in the door.

www.ccskills.org.uk/careers/advice/any/music

Find out more about the music industry and other creative industries in the UK.

www.thebigmusicproject.co.uk/how-to-find-work-experience-music-industry/

Learn more about how to get an internship in the music industry.

ABOUT THE AUTHOR

Mary Boone has been a freelance writer for nearly 20 years. She has written for magazines including *Entertainment Weekly* and *People* and has authored 30 non-fiction books for young readers on everything from boy bands and fashion designers to Midwest cooking and wild ponies. Mary and her family live in Tacoma, Washington, United States, where they enjoy crafts of all types and sizes.

WANT TO LEARN MORE ABOUT
THE CAREERS BEHIND THE SCENES
IN SOME OF THE WORLD'S MOST
GLAMOROUS INDUSTRIES?

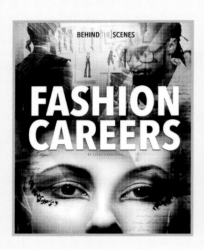 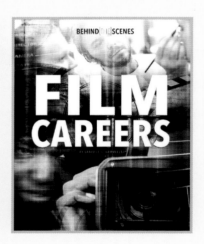

CHECK OUT THESE TITLES TO GO

Behind the Glamour

IN FASHION AND FILMS.